D0403687

spirit

These quotations were gathered lovingly but unscientifically over several years and/or contributed by many friends or acquaintances. Some arrived, and survived in our files, on scraps of paper and may therefore be imperfectly worded or attributed. To the authors, contributors and original sources, our thanks, and where appropriate, our apologies.—The editors

C R E D I T S

Compiled by Kobi Yamada
Designed by Steve Potter

ISBN: 1-888387-68-8

Printed in China

Exhilarate the spirit.

PHILLIP   MOWER

These are the days
of miracle and wonder.

PAUL   SIMON

It is absurd to say

that the age

of miracles is past.

It has not

yet begun.

OSCAR WILDE

Nature never

repeats herself,

and the possibilities of

one human soul will never

be found in another.

ELIZABETH CADY STANTON

JUST PUT
YOUR EAR DOWN
NEXT TO YOUR
SOUL
AND LISTEN HARD.

ANNE SEXTON

Spirit is like the wind, in that we can't see it but can see its effects, which are profound.

JIMMY CARTER

There is force in the universe, which, if we permit it, will flow through us and produce miraculous results.

MAHATMA GANDHI

Be strong, go with your heart, and believe in miracles because anything...anything can happen.

MARLO JAVIDANDO

I was always
looking outside myself
for strength and
confidence
but it comes
from within. It is
there all the time.

ANNA   FREUD

In the depth of winter, I finally learned that within me lies an invincible summer.

ALBERT CAMUS

In the face of

uncertainty there is

nothing wrong with hope.

O. CARL SIMONTON

Hope is a good thing,

maybe the best of

things, and no good

thing ever dies.

SHAWSHANK REDEMPTION

The human spirit is stronger than anything that can happen to it.

GEORGE C. SCOTT

The world breaks everyone and after-ward many are stronger in the broken places.

ERNEST HEMINGWAY

I count life
just as stuff to
try the soul's
strength on.

ROBERT BROWNING

Here lies the great gift of the spirit; though we may have lost our way, when we come to that realization, we discover the path once again.

DR. LAUREN ARTRESS

When you come to the edge

of all the light you have, and

must take a step into the

darkness of the unknown,

believe that one of two

things will happen. Either

there will be something

solid for you to stand on or

you will be taught how to fly.

PATRICK   OVERTON

Not knowing .

when the dawn

will come,

I open every door.

EMILY DICKINSON

TIS ALWAYS MORNING
 SOMEWHERE IN THE WORLD.

R I C H A R D   H E N R Y   H O R N E

Inside is a place where springs never dry up.

PEARL BUCK

Faith goes up the stairs

that love has built

and looks out the windows

which hope has opened.

CHARLES H. SPURGEON

Above all, watch with glittering eyes the whole world around you, because the greatest secrets are always hidden in the most unlikely places. Those who don't believe in magic will never find it.

RONALD DAHL

Only when we know
what is essential can
we know what is
possible. And the
wonder of it all is
that what is essential
is so vast and so
marvelous and what is
visible to the eye is so
limited and so small.

LEO BUSCAGLIA

Faith in small things has repercussions that ripple all the way out. In a huge, dark room a little match can light up the place.

JONI EARECKSON TADA

The ordinary acts we practice every day at home are of more importance to the soul than their simplicity might suggest.

THOMAS MOORE

We do not believe if we

do not live and work

according to our belief.

HEIDI WILLS

The thing
always happens
that you believe in;
and the belief
in a thing
makes it happen.

FRANK LLOYD WRIGHT

SOME THINGS HAVE TO BE BELIEVED TO BE SEEN.

MARK VICTOR HANSEN

Someday

all you'll have

to light the way

will be a single ray

of hope, and that

will be enough.

KOBI YAMADA

We can learn nothing

except by going

from the known

to the unknown.

CLAUDE BERNARD

I TRY TO LEARN FROM THE FINITE
THE LESSONS OF THE INFINITE.

ARTHUR YOUNG

There comes a time in the spiritual journey when you start making choices from a very different place. And if a choice lines up so that it supports truth, health, happiness, wisdom, and love, it's the right choice.

ANGELES ARRIEN

Strong is the soul, kind,
and wise, and beautiful.

MATTHEW ARNOLD

Real strength is

not just a condition of

one's muscle, but a

tenderness in

one's spirit.

M c C A L L I S T E R   D O D D S

MY RELIGION IS VERY SIMPLE.
MY RELIGION IS KINDNESS.

DALAI LAMA

Neither genius,
fame, nor love
show the greatness
of the soul.
Only kindness
can do that.

JEAN BAPTISTE

Each person has an ideal, a hope, a dream which represents the soul. We must give to it the warmth of love, the light of understanding and the essence of encouragement.

COLBY DORR DAM

Anytime we
catch a glimpse
of the soul,
beauty is there;
anytime we
catch our breath
and feel
"How beautiful!,"
the soul
is present.

JEAN SHINODA BOLEN, M.D.

The soul is here for its own joy.

RUMI

It is the soul's duty
to be loyal to its
own desires.
It must abandon
itself to its master
passion.

R E B E C C A   W E S T

...the more the

soul knows, the

more she loves,

and loving much,

she tastes much.

W. H. MURRAY

Whatever the soul

knows how to seek, it

cannot fail to obtain.

MARGARET FULLER

THERE IS ONE SPECTACLE

GRANDER THAN THE SEA,

THAT IS THE SKY; THERE

IS ONE SPECTACLE GRANDER

THAN THE SKY, THAT IS THE

INTERIOR OF THE SOUL.

VICTOR HUGO

There are incalculable resources in the human spirit, once it has been set free.

HUBERT H. HUMPHREY

Love really is the
answer. We're here
only to teach love.
When we're doing
that, our souls are
singing and dancing.

GERALD   JAMPOLSKY,   M.D.

We remember love in our hearts as the thing which, in life, made our hearts glad; we long for love in our souls as the thing that will carry us home.

DAPHNE ROSE KINGMA

WE ARE CITIZENS OF ETERNITY.

FEODOR DOSTOEVSKI

There will
come a time
when you believe
everything is finished.
That will be
the beginning.

After all, it is those who
have a deep and real inner
life who are best able
to deal with the irritating
details of outer life.

EVELYN UNDERHILL

Lightness enlightens.

JOEL GOODMAN

I BELIEVE IN THE ESSENTIAL UNITY

OF ALL THAT LIVES. THEREFORE,

I BELIEVE THAT IF ONE PERSON

GAINS SPIRITUALLY, THE WHOLE

WORLD GAINS, AND THAT IF

ONE PERSON FALLS, THE WHOLE

WORLD FALLS TO THAT EXTENT.

MAHATMA GANDHI

I got wings.

You got wings.

All God's children

got wings.

A F R I C A N   A M E R I C A N   S P I R I T U A L

You are an unrepeatable miracle.

DIANE ROGER

We may go to the moon,

but that's not very far.

The greatest distance

we have to cover

still lies within us.

CHARLES DE GAULLE

THE THINGS WHICH ARE NOT MEASURABLE ARE MORE IMPORTANT THAN THOSE WHICH ARE MEASURABLE.

ALEXIS CARREL

Those who make compassion an essential part of their lives find the joy of life. Kindness deepens the spirit and produces rewards that cannot be completely explained in words. It is an experience more powerful than words. To become acquainted with kindness one must be prepared to learn new things and feel new feelings. Kindness is more than a philosophy of the mind. It is a philosophy of the spirit.

ROBERT J. FUREY

To see the sunset

And then the night sky fill with stars

Is not half as beautiful to the eyes

As a dream is to the soul.

DAVID GETHINGS

the good life™

Celebrating the joy of living fully.

Also available from Compendium Publishing are these spirited companion books in The Good Life series of great quotations:

yes!
refresh
moxie
hero
friend
heart
success
joy
thanks

These books may be ordered directly from the publisher (800) 914-3327. But please try your local bookstore first!

www.compendiuminc.com